SOCIAL REVOLUTION AND CIVIL RIGHTS

AMERICAN ERAS: DEFINING MOMENTS

MARTIN GITLIN

Published in the United States of America by Cherry Lake Publishing Group
Ann Arbor, Michigan
www.cherrylakepublishing.com

Content Adviser: Kevin Whinnery, MA, History
Reading Adviser: Beth Walker Gambro, MS, Ed., Reading Consultant, Yorkville, IL
Photo Credits: © Photo by Warren K. Leffler/Library of Congress/LOC Control No. 2003654395, cover, 1;
   © Photo by Warren K. Leffler/Library of Congress/LOC Control No. 2003654393, 5; © Photo by
   Carol M. Highsmith/Library of Congress/LOC Control No. 2017880732, 7; © Photo by Marion S.
   Trikosko/Library of Congress/LOC Control No. 2003688130, 8; © Photo by Stanley Wolfson/Library
   of Congress/LOC Control No. 2005677031, 9; © Photo by Herman Hiller/Library of Congress/
   LOC Control No. 94505371, 10; © ZUMA Press Inc/Alamy Stock Photo, 13; © flickr/U.S. Embassy
   The Hague, 14; © Photo by Marion S. Trikosko/Library of Congress/LOC control No. 2003688129, 15;
   © Photo by Thomas J. O'Halloran and Marion S. Trikosko/Library of Congress/LOC Control No.
   2017646305, 16; © George Marks/istock, 19; © Tom Kelley Archive/istock, 20; © Photo by Warren K.
   Leffler/Library of Congress/LOC Control No. 2003673992, 21; © flickr/Equality Now, 22; © Photo
   by Thomas J. O'Halloran/Library of Congress/LOC Control No. 2011661233, 25; © Photo by Thomas
   J. O'Halloran and Warren K. Leffler/Library of Congress/LOC Control No. 2010646065, 26; © Osugi/
   Shutterstock, 28

Cherry Lake Press is an imprint of Cherry Lake Publishing Group.

Library of Congress Cataloging-in-Publication Data
Names: Gitlin, Marty, author.
Title: Social revolution and civil rights / by Martin Gitlin.
Description: Ann Arbor, Michigan : Cherry Lake Publishing Group, [2022] | Series: American eras:
   defining moments | Includes index.
Identifiers: LCCN 2021007824 (print) | LCCN 2021007825 (ebook) | ISBN 9781534187405 (hardcover) |
   ISBN 9781534188808 (paperback) | ISBN 9781534190207 (pdf) | ISBN 9781534191600 (ebook)
Subjects: LCSH: Social movements—United States—History—20th century—Juvenile literature. |
   Civil rights movements—United States—History—20th century—Juvenile literature. | Protest
   movements—
   United States—History—20th century—Juvenile literature.
Classification: LCC HN65 .G535 2022 (print) | LCC HN65 (ebook) | DDC 303.48/40973—dc23
LC record available at https://lccn.loc.gov/2021007824
LC ebook record available at https://lccn.loc.gov/2021007825

Cherry Lake Publishing Group would like to acknowledge the work of the Partnership for 21st Century
Learning, a Network of Battelle for Kids. Please visit http://www.battelleforkids.org/networks/p21
for more information.

Printed in the United States of America
Corporate Graphics

ABOUT THE AUTHOR

Martin Gitlin has written more than 150 educational books. He also won more than 45 awards
during his 11-year career as a newspaper journalist. Gitlin lives in Cleveland, Ohio.

TABLE OF CONTENTS

The popular notion is that Americans were content in the 1950s. That was only true for some.

Most White people were satisfied. Many had moved to comfortable homes in the suburbs. They were earning good money. Their families' lives were good. All was well.

But America was more than just White people. Most African Americans were neither happy nor content. They were unable to fulfill their dreams and goals. **Racism** and **discrimination** remained grim realities throughout the 1950s. They were roadblocks to success. That was especially true in the South.

Times were about to change as the 1960s arrived. Black Americans, with help from White people who fought alongside them, forced that change. They wanted their country to live out its creed that all people are created equal.

The 1960s brought many concerning issues to light.

The new decade was filled with violence and tragedy. In November 1963, President John F. Kennedy was **assassinated** as he rode in a motorcade in Dallas, Texas. Civil rights icon Martin Luther King Jr. was assassinated in April 1968. Kennedy's brother Robert was killed 2 months later as he campaigned for president. The United States was in turmoil.

By the late 1960s, protests and rebellions had broken out in many parts of the country. But many of these protests brought hope and opportunity to the African American community.

Sitting and Marching

The date was February 1, 1960. The city was Greensboro, North Carolina. The site was the lunch counter at the Woolworth store. There, four brave Black college students took a stand. They did so by sitting.

African Americans weren't allowed to sit at the lunch counter. But the students sat anyway. The four young men were refused service. But that didn't stop them. They came back the next day with other **activists**. The students began to receive national attention. They were beaten by racist people. But the young men refused to give in and leave. And it was worth it. Their protest worked. The lunch counter was **integrated** 5 months later.

College students Joseph McNeil, Franklin McCain, David Richmond, and Ezell Blair started a nationwide movement.

The civil rights movement was inspired by the courage of the protesters. Brave Black and White college students called the Freedom Riders went to work in 1961. They faced violence as they rolled into the deep South in buses to help end **segregation**.

The Freedom Riders began as a group of 13 people, including a young 19-year-old John Lewis.

Brave activists fought against the Jim Crow laws.
These were laws that allowed for racial segregation.

Activists were often beaten and arrested. One group was attacked while trying to integrate a bus terminal in South Carolina. Black protesters seeking the right to vote in Alabama were clubbed by police as they marched across a bridge. The admission of a Black student to the University of Mississippi caused a White riot on the campus.

The Civil Rights Act of 1964 made it illegal for public places and work environments to discriminate based on race, color, religion, sex, and national origin.

The spotlight on such events caused moral outrage. The result was positive change. President Lyndon B. Johnson signed the Civil Rights Act into law in 1964. That ensured all Americans had access to public places and ended job discrimination. He also signed the Voting Rights Act of 1965. That guaranteed all Americans the right to vote—regardless of skin color.

Such **legislation** brought greater freedom and equality. But African Americans weren't finished fighting for their rights. Some took a more **militant** approach as the 1960s progressed.

The March on Washington

The highlight of the civil rights movement occurred on August 28, 1963. That is when about 250,000 people from throughout the country gathered in Washington, D.C. They represented all races. But they spoke in a unified voice. They yearned to see an America free of racial discrimination. The event featured an inspiring speech by civil rights leader Dr. Martin Luther King Jr. He expressed his dream that one day the nation would live up to its ideals of equality. How much impact did the March on Washington make on the civil rights movement?

Taking a Violent Turn

Many African Americans embraced the methods of Martin Luther King Jr. in the 1960s. He preached nonviolent protest as a means to create change. Some Black people cited the Civil Rights Act and Voting Rights Act as proof that nonviolence was working.

But others claimed the pace of change was too slow. They still lived in **poverty**. Many remained stuck in northern **ghettos**. Some clashed with police, whom they felt treated them unfairly.

In 1967, hundreds of race riots happened across the United States. Pictured is the aftermath of a riot in Detroit, Michigan.

Anger boiled over in Black communities in the mid-1960s. The result was riots that caused death and destruction in major cities around the country. The violence was often sparked by small clashes with police. The most tragic riots occurred in 1967 in the cities of Detroit, Michigan, and Newark, New Jersey.

Martin Luther King Jr. believed that nonviolent protests, including marches, were the key to effective and lasting change.

Conflicts with the law weren't the cause of riots in April 1968. The assassination of Martin Luther King Jr. sparked violence in inner cities throughout the United States.

Some Americans blamed Black leaders for the rioting. But a study by the Kerner Commission cited poverty and hopelessness as the main cause.

[21ST CENTURY SKILLS LIBRARY]

The riots that followed Martin Luther King Jr.'s death were commonly referred to as the Holy Week Uprising.

"Never trust anybody over 30" was a popular saying
in the youth counterculture movement.

Inner-city riots finally ended in 1968. But the anger and
frustration that set them off would remain for generations.

African Americans weren't the only people seeking equal
opportunities in the 1960s. Women were also beginning to
fight for their rights.

The 1960s Youth Movement

There was another movement brewing: the emergence of the hippie **counterculture**. Many young Americans were taking a stand. They were finding ways to "stick it to the man" and rebel against "the establishment." These youths were called "hippies" or oftentimes "flower children."

These hippies wanted nothing to do with traditional norms. They were seeking change in every aspect. From the clothes they wore to the art and music they supported, the American youths were searching for freedom from tradition. Hemlines rose, which gave birth to miniskirts. The rise in Pop Art pushed "fine art" to the side. The Woodstock Festival in New York attracted over 500,000 of these peace-loving hippies. These youths believed that America had become too concerned with conformity, materialism, and competition. They valued tolerance, love, and nonviolent actions. What values are considered counterculture today? Who do you think the hippies are in today's modern world? Discuss your thoughts with a family member or friend. Ask them what they think.

The Women's Movement

About 6 million women joined the workforce during World War II. But most married women returned to their common role of housewives when the conflict ended.

That changed little during the next 2 decades. About one-third of all American women held jobs in 1950. The number had risen less than 10 percent by 1970.

Despite women joining the workforce during World War II, society in the 1960s still believed women only had one path in life: to be homemakers.

During the 1960s, women who worked were fairly limited to jobs such as teachers, secretaries, or nurses.

Yet the role of women had shifted greatly as the 1960s progressed. More women were seeking better jobs and higher pay. The **feminist** movement sought equality in all aspects of a woman's life. It was called the "second wave of feminism." The first wave was women's **suffrage**, which focused on the right to vote. The second-wave feminist movement focused on women's roles in the family and workforce.

The second-wave feminist movement included women from all walks of life, from young and old to upper- and lower-class backgrounds. But there were deep divides between the groups.

The FBI and CIA were so concerned about the feminist movement that they hired women to infiltrate the movement.

Women were undergoing a change in **perception** about their gender. That shift was promoted by the National Organization of Women (NOW). The group was founded in 1966. Among its stated goals for women was full participation in American society. NOW filed lawsuits against companies they believed didn't provide equal job opportunities to women.

The organization also pushed to change how women were viewed by others. One example was the annual Miss America beauty pageant. NOW **boycotted** the 1968 contest. It said that women shouldn't be judged by their outside appearances.

What had yet to be debated was whether women should serve as soldiers. But there was much debate in America during the 1960s about war.

A Breakthrough Book

The feminist movement of the 1960s was launched by a 1963 book written by Betty Friedan. It was titled *The Feminine Mystique*. The book criticized the typical roles women served as housewives and secretaries. It called for greater career opportunities for women. In later editions of the book, Friedan called for legalized **abortion**. That became a reality in 1973. Abortion remains a hotly debated topic. What are your thoughts about the debate between those for and against abortion? Use research to support your argument.

The Vietnam War

In the 1950s and 1960s, many Americans were worried about **communism**. The "domino theory" claimed that communism must be stopped in one country or it would spread to others, much like how one domino knocks over others in a row.

Americans were worried when Cuba adopted a Communist government in 1959. Their worries weren't unfounded. Three years later, the Communist **Soviet Union** placed missiles in that island country. The Soviet Union was the main rival to the United States' power at the time, and the two countries had very different ideas of how governments should work.

President Kennedy demanded that the Soviets remove the missiles. The world feared a nuclear war. But the Soviets backed down and removed the missiles.

More than 58,000 Americans and about 3 million Vietnamese lives were lost to the almost 20-year long Vietnam War.

The domino theory motivated President Lyndon B. Johnson to send American troops to fight a war in the Southeast Asian country of Vietnam. Vietnam was torn by a civil war that threatened to turn it entirely into a Communist country. South Vietnam had a democratic government, while North Vietnam was Communist. Many Americans couldn't even identify the country on a map. But by 1966, thousands of U.S. troops had already been killed there.

About 8.8 million men served in the United States military during the Vietnam War, and approximately 1.8 million men were drafted.

Soon, Vietnam wasn't the only nation that was torn. Americans became torn as well. Johnson's war policy became so unpopular that he refused to run for reelection in 1968. The **Tet Offensive** launched by North Vietnam early that year cast doubts about the U.S. military's ability to win the war.

About 500,000 U.S. soldiers were fighting in Vietnam by 1969. At that point, about half of the American people believed the war was wrong. Hundreds of thousands of people often gathered to protest the war. Some protests became violent.

[21ST CENTURY SKILLS LIBRARY]

The United States eventually drew down its involvement in Vietnam. But President Richard Nixon, who became president in 1969, continued Johnson's policy of bombing North Vietnam.

The war finally ended in 1975 when South Vietnam surrendered. Communism took over the entire country. The United States had lost a war for the first time in history. More than 58,000 American troops lost their lives. The Vietnam War would remain a topic of debate for decades to come. The United States' involvement in foreign wars became far more unpopular to the American people than they had been in the past.

During this time, another debate was brewing on American soil. The **environmental** movement was about to take off.

The Tragedy of Kent State

In May 1970, President Nixon expanded the Vietnam War into nearby Cambodia. Protests sprang up on college campuses throughout the country. Universities had been centers of antiwar feelings for several years. The war's expansion set off a firestorm at Kent State University in Ohio. On May 4, 1970, the National Guard, which had been called in to control the protests, fired into a crowd of protesters. Four students were killed. Research student's rights to gather and protest peacefully. Discuss your findings with a friend or family member.

Many social movements and revolutions started in the 1960s.

Research & Act

The 1960s was a decade of protest and social revolution. But African Americans and women weren't the only people fighting for their rights. A police raid at the Stonewall Inn in New York City in June 1969 set off rioting. The Stonewall was a bar frequented by gay people, who were forced by law to socialize in secret. With the help of a teacher or parent, research the Stonewall Riots to learn why gay people couldn't be open about their sexuality. What reasons were given by many Americans to suppress the gay community?

Timeline

February 1, 1960: The first sit-ins occur at the Woolworth lunch counter in Greensboro, North Carolina.

May 9, 1960: The U.S. Food and Drug Administration (FDA) approves use of the birth control pill, allowing women to control if and when they become pregnant.

November 8, 1960: John F. Kennedy defeats Richard Nixon in the presidential election.

May 4, 1961: The first Freedom Riders leave Washington, D.C., to work for integration in the South.

October 16–28, 1962: The Cuban Missile Crisis brings the world to the brink of a nuclear war.

August 28, 1963: Martin Luther King Jr. delivers his famous "I Have a Dream" speech during the March on Washington.

November 22, 1963: President Kennedy is assassinated in Dallas, Texas.

February 9, 1964: The rock-and-roll band the Beatles appear for the first time on American television. The "British Invasion" begins.

August 2, 1964: The Gulf of Tonkin incident motivates President Johnson to send American troops to Vietnam.

1965–1968: Riots bring death and destruction to many U.S. inner cities.

August 6, 1965: President Johnson signs the Voting Rights Act into law.

January 31–September 23, 1968: The Tet Offensive in South Vietnam sways opinions about American involvement in the war.

April 4, 1968: Martin Luther King Jr. is murdered in Memphis, Tennessee. Riots break out in many inner cities.

June 6, 1968: Presidential hopeful Robert F. Kennedy is assassinated after winning the California primary election.

November 5, 1968: Richard Nixon defeats Hubert Humphrey in the presidential election.

June 28, 1969: The Stonewall Riots in New York City bring attention to discrimination against gay Americans.

August 15–17, 1969: An estimated 500,000 young people gather in upstate New York to listen to their favorite rock artists at the Woodstock Festival.

October 15, 1969: An estimated 2 million Americans participate in protests against the Vietnam War.

Further Research

BOOKS

Gitlin, Martin. *Vietnam War*. Minneapolis, MN: ABDO Publishing, 2014.

Hoobler, Dorothy, and Tom Hoobler. *The 1960s: Rebels*. Minneapolis, MN: Millbrook Press, 2001.

Krull, Kathleen. *What Was The March on Washington?* New York, NY: Grosset & Dunlap, 2013.

WEBSITES

Ducksters—Civil Rights Act of 1964
https://www.ducksters.com/history/civil_rights/civil_rights_act_of_1964.php

National Geographic Kids—Hero for All: Martin Luther King, Jr.
https://kids.nationalgeographic.com/explore/history/martin-luther-king-jr

Glossary

abortion (uh-BOR-shuhn) medical termination of a pregnancy

activists (AK-tih-vists) people working toward social or political change

assassinated (uh-SAH-suh-nay-tuhd) when a well-known person is murdered, often for political reasons

boycotted (BOY-kott-uhd) refused to buy or use something on moral grounds

communism (KAHM-yuh-nih-zuhm) a system of government with single-party control of production

counterculture (KAWN-ter-kuhl-chur) a culture with values and morals that run counter to, or against, those of established society

discrimination (diss-krih-muh-NAY-shuhn) unfair treatment based on race or gender

environmental (en-VYE-ruhn-ment-uhl) having to do with the natural world of the land, sea, and air

feminist (FEH-muh-nist) person who believes in or works toward women's rights

ghettos (GEH-tohs) inner-city areas where people mainly of the same ethnic background or religion live

integrated (IN-tuh-gray-tuhd) something allowing people of different races to go to the same public places

legislation (leh-juh-SLAY-shuhn) laws made by a government

militant (MIH-luh-tuhnt) using strong or sometimes forceful measures to achieve a goal

perception (puhr-SEP-shuhn) an observation or opinion about something

poverty (PAH-vuhr-tee) the state of being poor

racism (RAY-sih-zuhm) negative treatment of people because of their race

segregation (seg-ruh-GAY-shuhn) the act of keeping people or groups apart

Soviet Union (SOH-vee-uht YOON-yuhn) a former federation consisting of Russia and a number of smaller countries

suffrage (SUHF-rij) the right to vote

Tet Offensive (TET uh-FEN-siv) a coordinated series of attacks by the Communist North Vietnam on the South Vietnamese people

INDEX